Excellent!

©Disney/Pixar

done!

©Disney/Pixar

Well
done!

©Disney/Pixar

Good
work!

©Disney/Pixar

I love
to read!

©Disney/Pixar

Well
done!

©Disney/Pixar

You
deserve a
reward!

©Disney/Pixar

STEPS TO READING

Dear Parent:

Congratulations! Your child is taking the first steps on an exciting journey. **The destination? Independent reading!**

STEPS TO READING will help your child get there. The programme offers three steps to reading success. Each step includes fun stories and colourful art, and the result is a complete literacy programme with something for every child.

Learning to Read, Step by Step!

(1) **Start to Read   Nursery – Preschool**
• **big type and easy words** • **rhyme and rhythm** • **picture clues**
For children who know the alphabet and are eager to begin reading.

(2) **Let's read together   Preschool – Year 1**
• **basic vocabulary** • **short sentences** • **simple stories**
For children who recognise familiar words and sound out new words with help.

(3) **I can read by myself   Years 1-3**
• **engaging characters** • **easy-to-follow plots** • **popular topics**
For children who are ready to read on their own.

STEPS TO READING is designed to give every child a successful reading experience. The year levels are only guides. Children can progress through the steps at their own speed, developing confidence in their reading, no matter what their year.

Remember, a lifetime love of reading starts with a single step!

By Dennis R. Shealy

This edition published by Parragon in 2011

Parragon
Queen Street House
4 Queen Street
Bath BA1 1HE, UK

ISBN 978-1-4454-2105-6

Printed in Malaysia

Disney · PIXAR

Race Team

PaRragon

Bath · New York · Singapore · Hong Kong · Cologne · Delhi
Melbourne · Amsterdam · Johannesburg · Auckland · Shenzhen

Lightning McQueen

is going to a race.

Mack will take him.

All the cars get ready.

Sarge and Flo bring

cans of gas and oil.

Guido loads Fillmore

with water for Lightning.

Guido packs spare tyres.

Mater drives in circles.

He is excited!

Mater cheers.

He wants Lightning

to win!

The pit crew is ready.

Lightning drives
to the starting line.
His pit crew yells,
"Go, Lightning, go!"

The cars drive
to the race.

It is far.

Poor Guido gets tired.

Mater gives him a tow.

Big trucks rest
at the truck stop.
The cars keep going.

Mater sees
Lightning and Mack.
There are cars
all around them.

Reporters ask Lightning

about the race.

They take many pictures.

The racetrack is a
busy place!
Mack parks in the pit.

He watches Lightning
practice.

Doc puts on his headset.

It is time for the race.

The race starts. <u>Vroom!</u>

Lightning is in front!

He drives the fastest.

Lightning gets tired.
But he keeps going.

Lightning McQueen

wins the race!

Ka-chow!

The race is over.
Lightning and Mack
head home!

Now turn
over for the
next story...

By Melissa Lagonegro
Illustrated by the Disney Storybook Artists

Disney·PIXAR

Snow Day

Bath · New York · Singapore · Hong Kong · Cologne · Delhi
Melbourne · Amsterdam · Johannesburg · Auckland · Shenzhen

It is Christmastime
in Radiator Springs!

Oh, what fun
the holiday brings!

Lightning and Sally
trim the tyre tree.

Mater hangs

lights carefully.

Flo serves oilcans
tied with bows.

Red has ribbons

on his fire hose.

Sarge leads

the group ahead.

Mater pulls
a big red sled.

Ramone paints stripes
on Lightning McQueen.

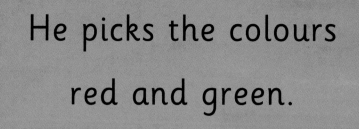

He picks the colours
red and green.

Lizzie sells stickers
to holiday buyers.

46

Luigi makes wreaths
from ribbons and tyres.

Cars drive home
after shopping all day.

Sheriff makes sure they
are stopping on the way.

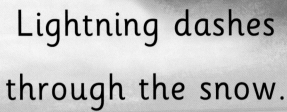

Lightning dashes
through the snow.

Mater is ready
if he needs a tow.

Guido shines

every snow tyre.

Sally warms up

over a fire.

Doc fills Sarge

with antifreeze.

Mistletoe makes

Mater sneeze.

Fillmore fills cars
with nice warm fuel.

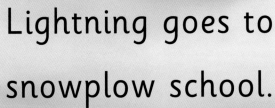

Lightning goes to
snowplow school.

The town is filled
with holiday cheer.

Christmas is
the best time of year!